THE MAGIC OF CLAY

Written and Illustrated by
Adalucia

Cholita Prints and Publishing Co.
Santa Fe, New Mexico

To Andrés,
the magical little person in my life

Very special thanks to Dr. Eric S. Cheney,
Associate Professor, Department of Earth
and Space Sciences, University of Washington,
Seattle, WA, for his helpful advice in preparing this book.

Special thanks to my editor Fernando Quan
and my graphic consultant Eduardo R. Quan.

Many thanks also to:
Debbie Samek Sontag, for teaching me to
love and respect clay.

And, my instructors and professors of ceramics:
Jane Kelsey-Mapel, Mesa Community College, Mesa, AZ

Kurt Weiser, Arizona State University, Tempe, AZ

Bill Gilbert, Gina Bobrowski, Michael Ceschiat,
and Kathryne Cyman,
University of New Mexico, Albuquerque, NM

—Adalucia

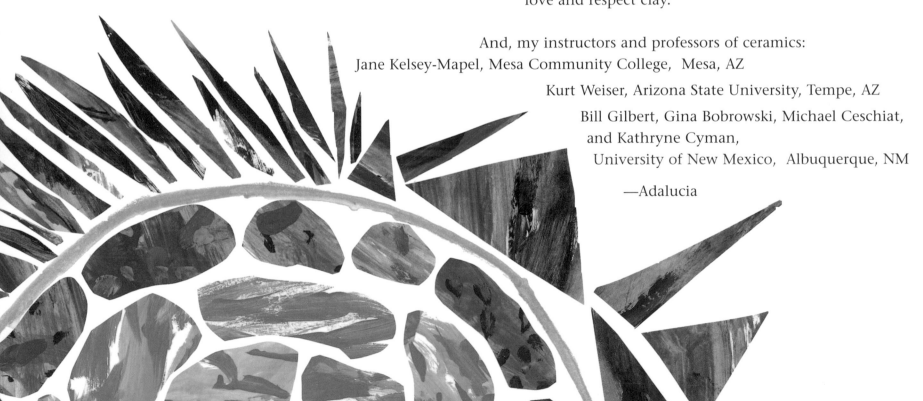

A long time ago our planet Earth got very, very hot. It was one bubbling mass of **magmas** or melted rocks. As our planet Earth cooled and the surface became **solid**, or hard, many minerals were formed. Minerals are the stuff rocks are made of.

And so, thousands of rocks were formed at this time.

Hi, I'm a special mineral called Feldspar. At one time, my mom and dad were igneous rocks.

More than half of the crust of the earth is made up of **Feldspar**, a special mineral found in most rocks. Most clays come from this very important mineral. **Granite** is the name of a rock with lots of feldspar.

In time, rain, wind, earthquakes and many other acts of nature, make these rocks break down and wear away. This is called **weathering**. From the breakdown or weathering of these rocks we get **clay**. Remember, this doesn't happen in a day or two. It takes millions of years for rocks to change and become clay. But because new rocks are forming all the time, clay is also forming all the time.

Igneous rocks were formed by the cooling of the magmas.

So
now we know
that clay comes
from
the Earth
and
from the Sky.

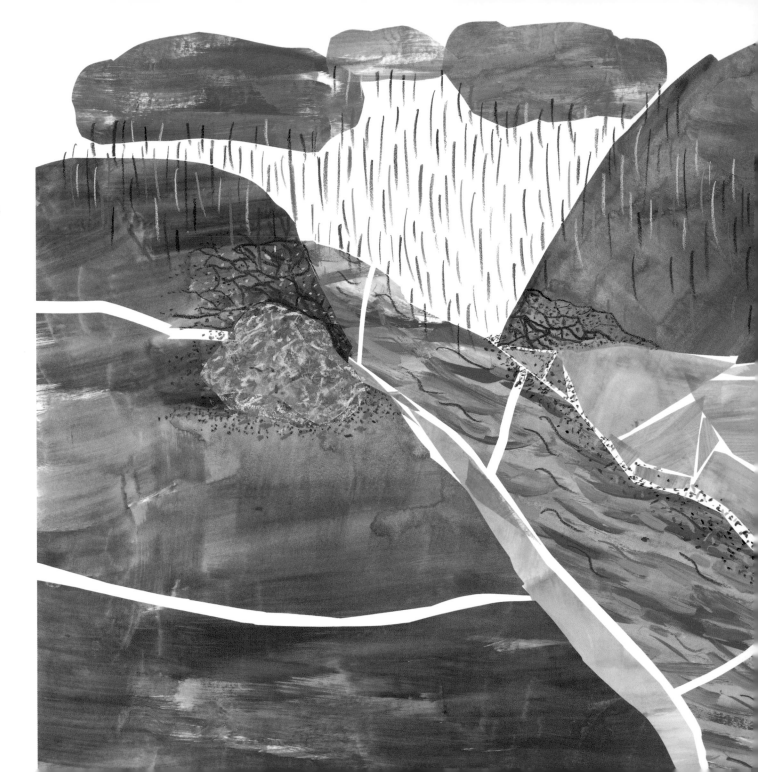

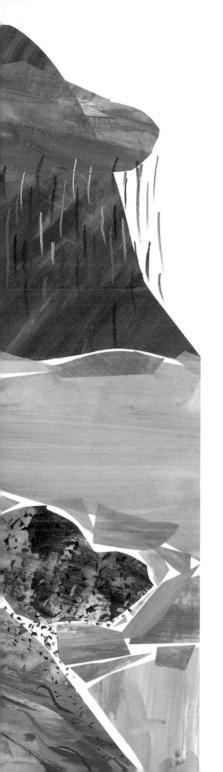

When rocks break down,
some of its components, like the salts, are carried away
by water from rain, rivers or **glaciers** (frozen masses).
This breakdown of our rocks takes years because it happens very slowly.
But in time, we are left with two very important materials, called by
their chemical names: **Alumina** and **Silica**.
Our rocks that started up in the mountain are now in the valley
all ground up and probably very wet.
The water that is in the ground is weathering our rocks. And the hotter the
water, the better. So, this water gets mixed up with the alumina and
silica from our rocks. Over the years, the water is stuck
together with these two materials in such a perfect way, that we say
this water is **chemically** combined.

CLAY

Now we have alumina, silica and water all stuck together. And do you know what this means? It means that we have **Clay**! Thanks to the water, our rocks have changed into clay.

This is the **formula** for clay:

$$Al_2O_3 \cdot 2SiO_2 \cdot 2H_2O.$$

A formula is the scientific or chemical way of describing a material.

Honey, Let's be friends.

O.K., friends forever!

We're water. Let's all be friends.

Hi, I'm Alumina.

Hi, I'm Silica.

Great!

Al_2O_3 alumina · $2SiO_2$ silica · $2H_2O$ water

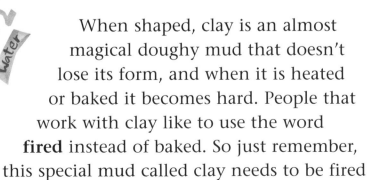

When shaped, clay is an almost magical doughy mud that doesn't lose its form, and when it is heated or baked it becomes hard. People that work with clay like to use the word **fired** instead of baked. So just remember, this special mud called clay needs to be fired to become strong.

Because minerals come in many colors, rocks come in a variety of colors and clay comes in different colors. We can find clay in shades of whites, yellows, grays, pinks, reds, and browns. Also, clay can have different **textures**. This means that to the touch some clays feel softer or rougher than others.

To understand clays better they are divided into two big groups: **Primary Clays** or clays that are in place and, **Secondary Clays** or transported clays. Primary Clays are clays that have been found on the rock or right next to the "mother" rock, and that's the place where they were formed. These clays are usually very white and pure. An example of a primary clay is **kaolin.**

Secondary Clays are clays that have traveled with the wind or the rivers, and have different colors. Sometimes these clays get a little "dirty" with the minerals, leaves or other things they pick along the way. All this not only changes the colors of clays but also the way they feel to the touch. This is all very good for the clay. It gives it different colors and textures. Some examples of these transported clays are the **surface** clays. We can often find these even in our own back yard, probably hidden under the top soil.

What is a Clay Body?

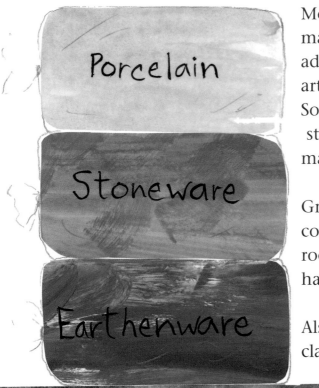

Porcelain

Stoneware

Earthenware

Most of the time other ingredients need to be added to the clay to make it easier to work with. **Natural** clay with other ingredients added is called a **clay body**. The three clay bodies that most clay artists use are: **porcelain, stoneware and earthenware**.
So clay needs a little help from us to make it a mushy but not so sticky material. Some potters add **fillers**, like sand and **grog**, to make their clay more workable.

Grog is the name given to tiny pieces of ground up, fired clay. It comes in different sizes or **meshes**. Grog can feel like miniature rocks, but it is really clay that may come from broken pots that have been crushed.

Also, it is important to add special "powders" called **flux**, so that clay can melt better. The mineral called feldspar is used as a flux. Bone ash, ground glass, salt, and other minerals can also be used as fluxes or melters.

Potters are always trying to come up with nicer clay bodies. They experiment by adding different things to their clay. You don't have to worry about making your own clay body. Already made, commercial clay bodies are sold at pottery supply stores and they have all the good stuff inside of them that makes them great to work with.

Potters that do **formulate** or make their own clay bodies need to be very careful and follow many safety rules, like using masks and gloves when mixing dry powders and other ingredients. It can be very bad for your lungs to breathe the clay "dust".

A **porcelain** clay body is very white and soft to the touch. When it is fired, it is very strong. Porcelain can sometimes be translucent. This means that a porcelain pot may let light show through and it can feel almost like glass.

Stoneware clay bodies come in many colors: grays, yellows, browns and even whites. Many potters that work **on the wheel** use this type of clay body. Ceramic pieces made out of stoneware look very sturdy. They may feel like a rock or stone. This is where stoneware gets its name.

If you find a clay pot in your patio, chances are it is an **earthenware** pot. Red earthenware is often called **terra cotta**. Earthenware is usually fired at much lower temperatures than stoneware or porcelain. This is why pieces made from earthenware may break and chip very easily.

Earthenware is a **low fire** clay body. Porcelain and stoneware are **high fire** clay bodies. Potters can make sculptures or **functional ware** from any of these three clay bodies.

Functional ware are things people use everyday like: cups, dishes, bowls, vases, and many other objects.

Clay is Plastic

Moist clay is elastic, but in ceramic terms we call it **plastic**. This is because the little particles that make up the clay are tiny and **hydrous**. Hydrous means containing water. So we say that clay is plastic because when it is damp, we can roll it into a coil, we can bend it and we can stretch it.

We can shape it into any form we like and it will stay this way even after it dries.

The most plastic of all clays is called **ball clay**.

This clay has moved in water a lot, and the particles in this clay are very tiny.

Tools

These are some of the basic tools you will need to work with clay.

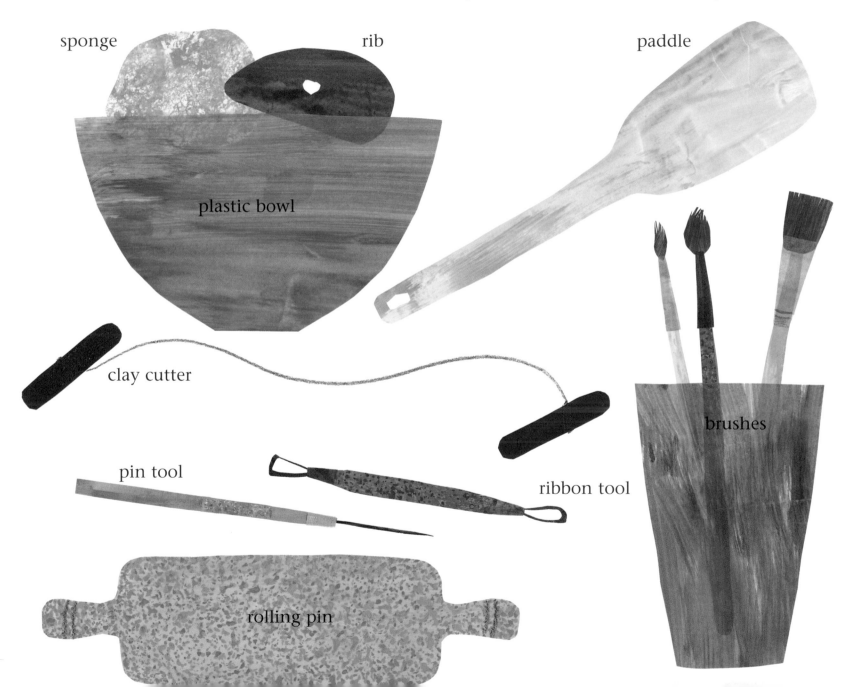

sponge

rib

paddle

plastic bowl

brushes

clay cutter

pin tool

ribbon tool

rolling pin

Clay needs to be wedged

The first thing we need to do to our clay is to knead it or to **wedge it**. Some potters cut and pound their clay to wedge it, others press it and rotate it in a spiral way. All this helps to make the clay even and easier to work with. But the main reason why clay needs to be wedged is to take out the air bubbles and lumps that could be inside. These air bubbles can trap the water in the clay. When this water gets hot during the firing, it changes to steam. This steam inside a bubble can make our clay pop and our pots can break or explode. When working with clay one thing you must always remember is that you cannot make any air pockets. If you are making a shape, which needs to be closed completely, it must always have a tiny hole for the air or steam to come out.

What is Leather Hard Clay?

Clay that has dried up a little and is stiff enough to be able to pick it up without messing up the shape is called **leather hard**.

Leather hard clay feels cool and damp. It looks darker than dry clay. This is because leather hard clay is still moist.

At this stage, we can reshape our bowls, make cuts, join corners and add decorations. Leather hard clay is nice for carving, too.

Ways of working with Clay

There are two basic ways of working with clay: **hand building**, and **using the potter's wheel**. One way of hand building clay is by **pinching** it. Another way is to use **slabs**, which are flat pieces of clay. Using **coils** or snake shaped forms is also a way of hand building.

Some potters like to make **molds** by pouring liquid clay called **slip** on plaster shapes. Molds are a fast way of making pots. You can stick hand built parts to mold pieces, or you can make little molds of animals, leaves, fruits, etc. Then you can attach these to hand built or **wheel thrown** pots or sculptures.

Wheel thrown is the term potters use when something is made on the potter's wheel.

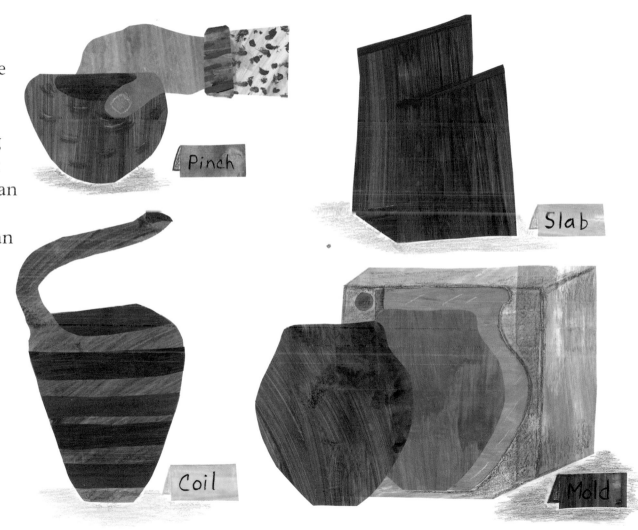

Pinch

Slab

Coil

Mold

What is Slip?

We said slip is liquid clay we can use to make molds. Slip can also be used as glue when we are attaching clay slabs or decorations. And, slip also makes your hands slide easier when working on the potter's wheel.
Slip really works as a **filler** when hand building. It helps you fill up all those little cracks and tiny holes you get when putting together slabs or coils.

Potter working on the wheel.

18

Slip and score are two words you will hear a lot. It just means you need to make crisscross lines in your clay using a fork or any other sharp tool. This is what scoring is all about. Then, you put the slip on the grooves that you have just made, and attach the parts. You must not forget to press with your fingers to make sure the pieces have stuck well. You can make slip by putting little chunks of clay in a bowl and covering them with water. After a while you will have the creamy liquid we call slip.

Some potters like to decorate their pots with colorful slips they make in their studios. They may add color to their white clay slip. These colors come as **stains** or **oxides**. You may also buy already made color slips called **underglazes**.

Oxides are ground up metallic minerals used just the way they are found in nature, in their raw state. These oxides may change their color during firing. An oxide that many potters like to use is red iron oxide. Oxides can be fired to high temperatures and some of them can give pots a shiny, metallic look.

Commercial **stains** are **pigments** that also come from minerals. They have already been fired and then reground, so they will not change their color during firing. Potters usually use these in low fire pieces.

What is Greenware?

All the clay pieces, before they are fired, are called **greenware.**

What does Bone Dry mean?

When most of the water from your greenware has dried up or **evaporated**, we say the clay is **bone dry**. Bone dry clay has a lighter color than a damp or leather hard piece. A bone dry piece really does feel like a bone and this is where it gets its name. Bone dry clay can break very easily, so you need to be extra careful when touching or handling your pieces at this stage.

Put a pot against your cheek. How does it feel? Cool and wet, or dry and not so cold? If it feels dry, it is ready to be fired because your piece is now bone dry.

Where is Clay fired?

Clay is usually fired in very hot ovens called **kilns**. There are two kinds of kilns: **electric** kilns and **fuel burning** kilns.

Two important fuel burning kilns are: gas and wood kilns.

Potters all over the world fire their pots and sculptures in many different ways. Some potters don't even use kilns.

This picture shows the different ways in which potters fire their pieces or **ware**.

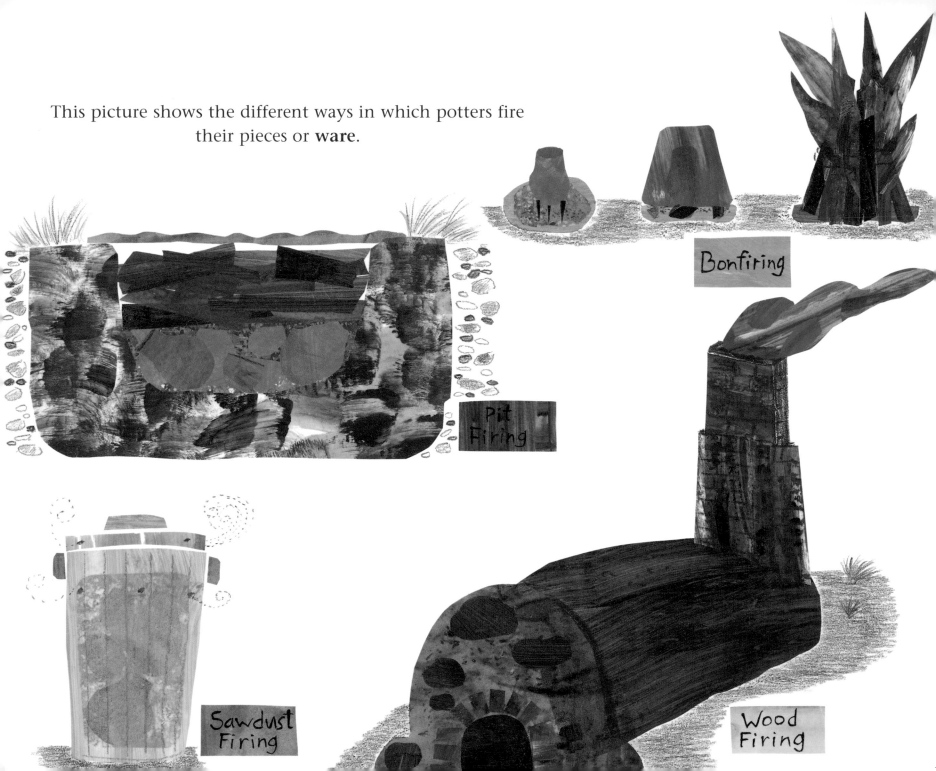

Bonfiring

Pit Firing

Wood Firing

Sawdust Firing

What is a Cone? Δ

A cone is a little triangular shaped object made of clay materials. This cone bends when the kiln gets hot enough. A potter can tell when the kiln has reached a certain temperature because the cone has bent. So cones are used inside the kilns to know how hot the kilns are. Also, cones are used to shut off the electric kilns that are fired manually. Cones come in different sizes and they also have different colors, depending on the temperature they are meant to bend at.

Nowadays potters can use computerized kilns that are very modern and do not use cones. But these kilns, like old-fashioned manual kilns, are not meant to be fired fast. It takes a long time to fire a kiln because the clay goes through many changes when it is being heated. If a potter tries to fire fast, the pieces can break or explode.

Also, when potters need to talk about temperature, they usually talk about "cones". A pot fired to cone 10 or cone 6 is high fire. A piece fired to cone 04 or cone 06 is low fire. The chart shows the temperatures of a few cones:

Cone 10	——	1305° C
Cone 6	——	1222° C
Cone 1	——	1154° C
Cone 04	——	1060° C
Cone 06	——	999° C

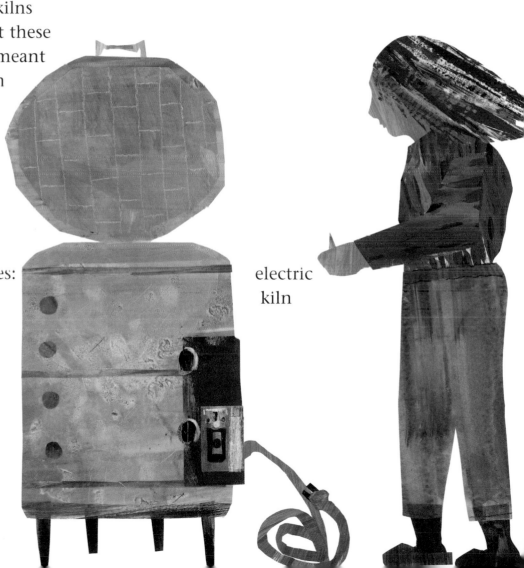

electric
kiln

What is Bisque Ware?

Fired pieces are now called **bisque** pieces or **bisque ware**.

Bisque pieces are no longer plastic, they are no longer damp, leather hard or bone dry. They are now strong. They are now **ceramic**. A ceramic pot can never go back to being a soft pot. Usually potters do a bisque firing to make their clay hard, porous and ready for the next step.

The word porous only means that the clay particles have not yet joined together really tight so the bisque piece has a rough texture.

Now the piece is ready to be painted or **glazed**. The special "paints" that potters use are called **glazes**. The rough texture of their bisque pieces will help these glazes stick better.

Clay shrinks

Clay shrinks when it changes from the moist stage, to leather hard, to bone dry. Clay shrinks even more after a bisque fire. This is because all the water, even the chemical water, the clay had inside has evaporated. The little particles inside the clay have **fused** or joined together more tightly with the firing. Following a high temperature **glaze firing** a pot will get a lot smaller and the little particles will have joined together even more.

Glazes

Glazes can make any pot or sculpture beautiful. One thing to remember about glazes is that they must shrink with our clay so that they may have a perfect fit. This is why we need to use the glazes that match our clay body. There are high fire glazes and low fire glazes.

Glazes can be very colorful or they can be **transparent**. This means they are usually clear and can let light shine through. Glazes can also be bright or dull, shiny or matt. Oxides used in glazes can give you many different colors that may change depending on the type of firing. For example, cobalt gives you blue. Manganese gives you purple or brown and copper can give you shades of greens or reds. Potters that fire in fuel burning kilns can adjust the air (or oxygen) in these kilns. They usually "starve" their kilns of air at a certain temperature so that the oxides in the glazes can change their colors. This is called **reducing** a kiln or **firing in reduction**. When you fire in an electric kiln, we say you fire **in oxidation**. This is because there is oxygen inside the kiln all the time.

BEFORE Firing

AFTER Firing

Potters use different ways of glazing.

Low fire glazes are usually painted on with a brush or sponge.

CLEAR Glaze

GREEN Underglaze

RED Underglaze

When using high fire glazes, the pots are dipped inside big buckets of glaze. A potter can use his hands or tongs to dip his pieces. The glaze can also be poured inside the pot or splattered around to make fun designs. The glaze firing, which is usually the last firing, is very important because glazes make pots very **durable**. Glazes also make pots **impermeable**.

This means that water cannot leak through. So any functional piece like a cup or bowl, for example, that is meant to be used to drink or eat from, should have glaze.

It is not good for children to work with glazes because some of the ingredients could be toxic. They can use non-toxic paints to decorate their pots and their ceramic pieces will still be beautiful.

Clay is Fragile

This means clay pieces can break very easily. So we need to be extra careful when touching or handling our clay.

Clay is Timeless

Clay is a very old piece of our earth. We say it is **timeless** because we will always have clay. Handmade clay pieces are special. They are precious because they are unique. So we should handle all clay pieces with much care, out of respect for the person who made them.

The wonderful thing about clay is that it can show not only what great artists our ancient potters were, but also many pots tell stories of the way people lived long ago.

Clay is a timeless,
almost magical material
that lets you change a lump of our earth
into a beautiful object.

Black-on-red
vase
GREECE, 540 B.C.

MOCHICA vessel
PERU,
A.D. 200-500

MIMBRES bowl
southwestern U.S.A.,
A.D. 950

ARITA ware
JAPAN,
17th Century

"Listen to your clay,

Feel its magic

and

Create."

—Adalucia

Published by:
Cholita Prints & Publishing Co.
P.O. BOX 8018
Santa Fe, NM 87504
cholitaprints@comcast.net

ISBN 0-9742956-0-4
Library of Congress Control Number
2003093968

The text and illustrations of this book have been checked for accuracy by experts in the fields of geology and ceramics. Every effort has been made to ensure that all the information printed in this book is correct.

Printed in Hong Kong